Word Sparks

Active Meditations from God's Word

JENNI BUTZ

TheWordSpark.com

Word Sparks

Word Sparks – TheWordSpark.com

All rights reserved. No part of this book may be reproduced or transmitted in any form or by any means, electronic or mechanical including photocopying, recording or by any information storage or retrieval system, without the written permission of the publisher, except where permitted by law.

Limit of Liability: While the author and the publisher have used their best efforts in preparing this book, they make no representation or warranties with respect to accuracy or completeness of the content of this book. The advice and strategies contained herein may not be suitable for your situation. Consult with a professional when appropriate.

Copyright © 2015 by Jenni Butz

Published by Pacelli Publishing
9905 Lake Washington Blvd. NE, #D-103
Bellevue, Washington 98004
Pacellipublishing.com

ISBN-10: 1508639108
ISBN-13: 978-1508639107

Word Sparks

צוֹצִין

(nee-TSOHTS) means *spark* in the physical sense, but
the word is used far more often to refer to that
spark of life, what some might call a divine spark,
within us all--without exception.
(*Your Daily Dose of Hebrew*,
Ami Steinberger)

What you're about to read is a compilation of epiphanies, big and small, that God has given to me over the years. There is the divine all around us in the everyday; all we need to do is look. Once we begin to train our minds to connect the dots between all the miraculous, poignant, devastating, and ordinary circumstances of our lives, the conclusion can only be that the Master Weaver is making a beautiful tapestry out of it all for His glory. Some entries will ask questions to prompt further thought or prayer. Some will merely nudge you closer to a direction where God may already be leading you. My hope is that as you read, you will pause just long enough to allow God's Spirit to reveal Himself to you in new ways. Use this as a resource for slightly deeper conversations. Use it as a springboard for journaling or further Bible study. Heck, I don't even care if you use it to kill time while you're in the bathroom! Just think and pray and reflect. God will do the rest.

Acknowledgements

Because every good and perfect gift comes from the Father of the heavenly lights, I want to thank you, Lord, for the gifts of your Spirit. Thank you for your body, the church. Without those valuable friends, I wonder if I would have written a word for anyone else to read. Thank you for my EPIC girls, who are always the first to read and comment on whatever you put on my heart to write. Thank you for a mom and a dad who have always believed I was a rock star. And thank you for a husband and son who inspire and encourage me to think about you and life differently.

Also by Jenni Butz

Building in Times of Peace: An Inductive Bible Study

Table of Contents

Sun in the Trees 9

Get it Out! 13

Paul's Example 17

Jesus Christ Superstar 19

Scavenger Hunt 23

Weighing In and Mandatory Retirement 25

Confidence 29

Work and Play 31

Building a Kingdom 35

Naaman 39

The Cross on the Side of the Road 41

Conviction 45

Toilets, Lies, and Humility 51

A Crown 55

Fear and Splendor 59

Whose Honor? 65

Conversations 69

He is Risen! 73

Evil 75

Dilemma 81

Invitations 87

Word Sparks

Battling Sloth 97

Diagnosis or Cure? 101

"Your Majesty" 109

Candy Hoarder 113

Fully Equipped 117

Big Leaf, Little Leaf 121

Responding to God 125

Mountaintop Experiences 133

No Longer a Burden 139

Setting The Pace 141

City Moses and Desert Moses 145

Sun in the Trees

> "From where I lay I can see the sun,
> rising through the trees.
> Before I face this morning rush,
> I get down on my knees.
>
> I lift my eyes and I thank you
> for this life you've granted me.
> I pray that every day I live,
> your heart will be pleased."
>
> (from *All I Ever Wanted*, by Margaret Becker)

I was thinking of this old favorite song of mine one morning, as I sat watching the sun peek through the trees on its way to light the sky for the day. I was reading about the land allotments in the book of Joshua and paused to stretch my problematic neck.

I caught a momentary glimpse of bright orange as the rising sun peeked through the cedars in the backyard. In that split second, I sensed God saying to me, as He had to Paul centuries ago,

"My grace is sufficient for you, for my power is made perfect in weakness." (2 Corinthians 12:9)

Word Sparks

Recently, I've been struggling with an ongoing personal issue and, even though I was stretching for physical comfort in that moment, God met me with a much deeper comfort. A reminder that although it only seems we see the sun for a second, it's always there. Even though there may only be a spot--a single ray--of sunlight shining into our darkness, it's never blotted out completely.

God's light--His comfort, His truth, His love--is always rising to fill our lives.

Whether we see the effects dimly--diffused through leaves or morning fog--or if it's brilliantly spectacular in its hues and intensity, the sun--like God--is constant and unchanging. We'll catch glimpses; then it will seem to disappear because we've lost sight of it. But God will use His Word, His Spirit, and other people in our lives to remind us that He is there.

As I sat and saw the shadows and lighting shift among the trees, I was reassured. I sensed God's peace in my present situation as well as for life in general, as He reminded me that His grace IS sufficient for me. Whether I need to pull up my big girl panties and suck it up because life just feels hard right now, or I lay out my heart before Him in my need and pain, what He offers is enough.

Word Sparks

Get it Out!

"These muscles are angry." Words spoken by my chiropractor as she delved deeply into my shoulder tissue, stretching my neck while massaging tender places on the opposite side.

This, after I had taken a deep breath in, lying on my stomach, and let it out slowly, only to have her hands come down powerfully in the middle of my back, releasing an audible, unwitting "HUH!" from my lips.

Why would anyone submit to this treatment?!

Because whatever Dr. Denniston does is for my good. (Anyone see where I'm going with this?)

Most of us don't want God or other people poking and prodding in our lives, especially when it reveals something uncomfortable or downright sinful. Conversations with friends that push back on my bad theology or question my motivations and behaviors are unpleasant. God's Word shining its objective light into the dark recesses of my conscience can illuminate areas of my life that aren't holy. Sometimes it's unpleasant;

sometimes it's painful.

But what's the goal of opening ourselves up to the scrutiny and treatment of those we trust? Hopefully our goal is wholeness and health. Nothing short of transformation.

Jesus told the religious leaders of His time: *"You have let go of the commands of God and are holding on to the traditions of men."* (Mark 7:8) That could not have been easy to hear, especially because the rebuke was so public. Jesus was exposing the wrong motivation of their hearts: they were all about themselves and not about God. Ouch.

So the reason I seek out the objective truth of God's Word and the authentic conversations of trusted friends is because I want that stuff out of me! I want and need help seeing my personal blind spots, even if it's uncomfortable. Even if it makes me angry and defensive at first. Because in the process of examining truth in the inmost parts (Psalm 51), I move forward in the transformation process of becoming more like Jesus. And in understanding Him more and more.

Word Sparks

And as I've discovered in chiropractic care, sometimes things have to get worse before they can get better. Adjusting one area that's out of alignment requires that our whole bodies make the shift and feel the brunt of the change. But there are devastating effects of vertebral subluxation if we allow the misalignment to continue. (Right, Dr. D?)

Lord, open my heart to the unerring truth of your Word, the clear and powerful conviction of your Holy Spirit, and the trusted words of friends who love me like you do. Would you do whatever it takes to align me with your will to reflect your glory to the world around me? Amen.

Word Sparks

Paul's Example

One summer a few years ago, I was reading through Philippians and Colossians with some of my girlfriends on Facebook. The week we read Philippians 4 I was struck by the repetition of Paul's bold invitation to follow his example in following Christ. Here, he says it in verse 9:

"Whatever you have learned or received or heard from me, or seen in me--put into practice. And the God of peace will be with you."

In verse 17 of Chapter 3 he said:

"Join with others in following my example, brothers, and take note of those who live according to the pattern we gave you."

What would that look like in those lives I've discipled if they followed my example and put into practice not only what they've learned, received, and heard from me, but also what they've *seen*? Definitely better some days than others. Paul was so intentional about having those people in his life, wasn't he? He constantly multiplied himself by investing in younger men to further the kingdom.

Have you been the beneficiary of that kind of relationship? Have you had the blessing of being that example to someone else? It's quite a challenge, but also very satisfying. It requires that we spend a lot of time with God, allowing Him to make us into an example that can be followed. And an example that always points back to Jesus. Lord, let it be so.

Who are some people who have been an example to you, showing you what it means to follow Christ? To whom are you trying to be that example? Take a few moments to think about some people who have been an example to you and those to whom you may be an example. Then thank God and ask for His wisdom and guidance in these relationships.

Jesus Christ Superstar

I remember clearly the night our family and some friends saw a local production of *Jesus Christ Superstar.* Having never seen the production, I had been warned that it might be offensive, and some actually used the word blasphemous. I am publicly admitting today that I am either theatrically ignorant or more religiously tolerant than I thought. Or both.

In bullet points (because it's how I think and see the world) here are my observations:

- No one approaches the subject of Jesus' life without bringing a certain bias, and Andrew Lloyd Weber and Tim Rice are no exception. They are entitled to express their bias with their own creative and brilliant methods.
- The music of the 70's rocked!
- There is no biblical evidence for portraying Mary Magdalene as a woman with a sordid sexual past, but there it was. Again, I refer to my first point: you're the genius in theater--you get to portray

the characters any way you like. Weber and Rice were certainly not the first, nor will they be the last, to think of Mary as a former whore.

- Dan Brown (author of *The DaVinci Code*) probably loved this play. The whole Mary/Jesus love connection...I'm just sayin'.

- Jesus and Judas did die the same week. Fascinating premise to chronicle what that last week would have been like between them. (Also wondering how that era produced such high tenors that could melt your face with their singing. Who knew that's what Jesus and Judas had in common?)

- Staging the tongue in cheek numbers (think Herod in a spa and Judas in the all-sequined afterlife) just that way seemed apt in light of how off everyone was in their assessment of Jesus' purpose. Had Jesus jumped down off the cross to appease the crowd's thirst for sensationalism, everyone would have believed; but they would have believed in an incomplete Jesus. Bottom line: He had to die and rise to actually conquer sin and death. It wasn't the show-stopping number everyone anticipated. It was so much more. I miss it too, sometimes. "Prove you're who you say you are," I demand. As if this life is about me.

- I don't believe Jesus told the lepers, the lame, the poor, and the blind to heal themselves, as He did in the play, but I do believe He may have felt tempted to, if we're to believe Hebrews 4:15, which tells us that "*we do not have a high priest who is unable to sympathize with our weaknesses, but we have one who has been tempted in every way, just as we are--yet was without sin.*"

- The song Jesus sang in the Garden of Gethsemane scene depicts every bit of anguish and desperation that I picture when I read the gospels. Gorgeous lyrics, heartbreaking delivery. What must that night have been like? Did it feel like Jesus was drinking poison to obey? How does that figure in with the description in Hebrews 12 that says Jesus endured the cross "for the *joy* set before him"? And what would it be like for me to have my mind so focused on an eternal perspective--so consumed with love for my Savior--that joy could be mingled with anguish? I think I've experienced that to some degree in my life at times, but nothing like Jesus.

So I think the 1973 movie might have to move up on my Netflix list. Those rockin' disciples and their songs are going to be haunting me for a while.

Scavenger Hunt

My son's youth group did a scavenger hunt at church when he was in middle school.

I didn't ask him the kinds of things they were supposed to look for but I have been thinking about my own hunt, as I scavenge (is that even a word?) through life looking for purpose. Looking for God's glory. For comfort. Love. Beauty.

Is there holiness in raising my face to the sun and letting it dry the tears that stream down my cheeks, escaping my tightly squeezed eyelids?

Is there holiness in sitting at my desk, reaching for the words to describe God's truth, and being distracted by a huge spider that meanders, uninvited, along the baseboard, among electrical cords?

Is God's glory in snoring spouses?

Is there something divine in stitches from surgery and post-op meds that are instantly bitter on the tongue but stave off infection in the body?

Word Sparks

My theology is challenged in the dichotomy of the divine and the mundane.

Yes, God is present in all of it. He made the sun's warmth. The unwelcome arachnid is His creation, too. (Ew!) He's in the nearness of noisy breathing. In the healing process. In my triumphs and in my epic fails.

He is everywhere and in everything.

And He wants to be found. To be seen. To be embraced and sought after.

This is my scavenger hunt list:

One thing I ask of the LORD,
this is what I seek:
that I may dwell in the house of the LORD
all the days of my life,
to gaze upon the beauty of the LORD
and to seek him in his temple. (Psalm 27:4)

Reveal yourself to me, Lord. Show me your beauty and your glory in everything today. Amen.

What do you want to ask God to reveal to you?

Weighing In and Mandatory Retirement

It's time for Numbers in my trek through the Bible. For many, it's a book for skimming. And while there's a place for that, I'm noticing some fascinating details in this book of many details this time around.

And instead of my usual researching and pondering to find the answers to my periodic "huh?" I'm going to pose the questions to you, since I'm going to bet you skimmed this part the last time you read the 7th and 8th chapters of the book of Numbers.

Numbers 7 describes each tribe of Israel giving an offering for the newly consecrated Tent of Meeting. This is what each of the 12 tribes brings:

12 The one who brought his offering on the first day was Nahshon son of Amminadab of the tribe of Judah.

13 His offering was one silver plate weighing a hundred and thirty shekels and one silver sprinkling bowl weighing seventy shekels, both according to the sanctuary shekel, each filled with the finest flour mixed with olive oil as a grain offering; 14 one gold dish weighing ten shekels, filled

Word Sparks

with incense; 15 one young bull, one ram and one male lamb a year old for a burnt offering; 16 one male goat for a sin offering; 17 and two oxen, five rams, five male goats and five male lambs a year old to be sacrificed as a fellowship offering. This was the offering of Nahshon son of Amminadab.

Each of the other tribes then brings *exactly the same thing* as an offering. So, here's my question:

Where did these wandering Jews in the desert get all this gold and silver when they ran for their lives in the middle of the night of Passover?

I think I have the answer to this, which highlights God's attention to detail, but what do you think?

Personally, I see this as an example of a pattern I've discovered in Scripture: God provides the very thing He asks us to give back to Him. What if these precious items came from Exodus, when the Hebrews took all kinds of booty from their Egyptian neighbors? God gave it to them, so they could give it right back. I love it.

Second "huh?" moment is in chapter 8:

Word Sparks

23 The LORD said to Moses, 24 "This applies to the Levites: Men twenty-five years old or more shall come to take part in the work at the tent of meeting, 25 but at the age of fifty, they must retire from their regular service and work no longer. 26 They may assist their brothers in performing their duties at the tent of meeting, but they themselves must not do the work. This, then, is how you are to assign the responsibilities of the Levites."

Mandatory retirement age is in the Bible! What? The Levites have to retire from duty on the tabernacle when they turn fifty. Why do you suppose that is?

Could it be that after a season of serving God in one capacity, it's time for fresh perspective? Maybe the Levites weren't meant to cease working altogether, but just shift their energies and attentions to another way of serving, using their life experience to enrich others.

Sometimes Scripture just makes me say, "Huh."

Word Sparks

Confidence

"'This is what the great king, the king of Assyria, says: On what are you basing this confidence of yours?'" (2 Kings 18:19)

This is a question I've been pondering a lot over the past year or so. On what am I basing this confidence of mine?

If it was on my looks, then middle-age is taking care of changing that.

If it's on my smarts, well, God Himself took that off the table by endowing me with only slightly above average intellect.

On doing the right thing? Good luck to those around me. I score a "zero" on the scales of compassion and service.

How about my accomplishments? Again, not much to brag about.

It would be pretty easy to look at me and say, "On what are you basing this confidence of yours?"

But what if, like Hezekiah, I'm basing my confidence

on God's promises? What if I believed what God said is true regardless of what anyone else says about me or my chances of success in this world?

Because God says I'm loved.

I'm redeemed and forgiven.

And I was chosen to be adopted into His family.

And that He's got my back and is preparing a place for me to spend eternity with Him.

So in spite of my lack of credentials or achievements, in the face of colossal mistakes and epic fails, I am pretty confident. Not in me, of course, but in the God who chose me, loves me, and calls me to live for Him.

What are you basing your confidence on? What is God saying to you about that?

Work and Play

I just got home from Paris.

Don't feel too badly for me. It wasn't as bad as it sounds.

We had good food, walked for miles, ate crêpes in the Tuileries Gardens, and took a fascinating tour of the Veuve Clicquot champagne cellars. All in all, a pretty rocking week.

But have you discovered that no matter how glorious the vacation, how amazing the scenery, and how fascinating the experience, once you know it's time to get home, you just can't wait?

What is that?

I have a theory.

It's time to be productive. It's how we were designed.

Take a look at this verse from the creation account:

"The LORD God took the man and put him in the Garden of Eden to work it and take care of it." (Genesis 2:15)

And this one from a wise, wise king:

"Then I realized that is it good and proper for a man to eat and drink, and to find satisfaction in his toilsome labor under the sun during the few days of life God has given him--for this is his lot." (Ecclesiastes 5:18)

We were meant to live in a balance of work and pleasure. Labor and laughter. Toil and tranquility.

And often we don't realize we lack one because we're so imbalanced in the other.

I've recently taken on some tutoring responsibilities, getting my feet back into the world of education, and it wasn't until my days were filled with meaningful activities that I realized how much time I had been wasting! There is great satisfaction in doing a job and doing it well.

We were created with a rhythm and a tension. It's the concept behind God's emphasis over and over again on the Sabbath. Work your tails off for six days, then take a break, for crying out loud! A real break that changes pace, focus and priority. Then go back to what you were doing with God at the center of it.

Word Sparks

Recalibration is good because it realigns our purposes and priorities. And in my opinion, there are few places better to do that than Paris with a few girlfriends.

But now it's time to be productive again. Bring it on, Lord!

Word Sparks

Building a Kingdom

I have to come clean and admit that I'm fully engaged in a Facebook game called Castleville. (Here's a shout-out to all my friends in neighboring kingdoms who have been so kind as to visit me and give me shards of exploration crystals and have unwithered my crops. Hollah....)

The tagline on this highly addictive and relatively unproductive game is: *Build a happy kingdom with your friends.* How could I resist? I mean, who doesn't long to build a happy kingdom with friends? I want a kingdom, of which I am presumably in charge, and I want to have community. So it's perfect, right?

Sure, if all you have to do is complete random quests given to you by Rafael and Yvette by chopping down trees, crafting in your workshop, and destroying beasties who invade your happy kingdom. Then you are set.

However, as I've been contemplating deeper, more spiritual questions, the tagline of Castleville has been reverberating in my mind. As my family and friends have been through some tough church issues in the past few years, I find myself asking the question: what's church for? The realization I've come to is that for most of my adult life I've thought church is to build a happy kingdom with my friends.

It's not.

I heard a fantastic sermon at church once entitled: *"Life at 2 a.m.--Why are we here?"* Our purpose in life is to glorify God, and when we do that in community we build HIS kingdom, not ours. And whether or not our friends are there, we love others and work together in unity to work toward HIS purposes, doing HIS will. It's not about us.

Church is not about building our kingdom with our friends. It sounds obvious, but isn't that how we react when things go badly? Is it manifested in our priorities in such a way that we live in a tension between our individual surrender to God's Spirit and our devoted participation in His body?

The temptation is great to work toward building a happy kingdom with my friends. But the bottom line is that my friends aren't always around and they often have very little to do with what God is asking me to do to build His kingdom.

Friends move away; God is always with us.

Friends disappoint us; God is always faithful.

Friends are sinners; God is holy and just.

This personal epiphany has opened my eyes to a new perspective and I'm hoping God will continue to show me how He wants to use me to build His eternal kingdom. I sure would love company if you're up for it.

Word Sparks

Naaman

"Go wash yourself seven times in the Jordan and your flesh will be restored and you will be cleansed."

But Naaman went away angry and said, "I thought he would surely come out to me and stand and call on the name of the LORD his God, wave his hand over the spot and cure me of my leprosy." (2 Kings 5:10-11)

Am I missing out on something God wants to do in my life because I'm too focused on the expectations I've built up? Is my focus on the wrong thing so I don't see God's activity in my life? Do I want drama more than His Presence? And can I even clearly identify my need?

My expectations?

My hope?

Am I, like Naaman, expecting God to do something big in my life while I wait, idly, and simply complain?

That's not what I want, Lord! I want to respond by doing whatever you require of me; just show me what it is! Oh, that it would be as clear as it was for Naaman. But then, would I balk like he did? Probably.

As is true so often in Scripture--and in life--there is a tension that exists between what only God can do and what He asks me to do. How could I possible get those confused?

But I do.

Would you give me eyes to see the difference, Lord? And strength to act or submit, accordingly.

How would you weigh your expectations in a current life situation you're facing with how God has responded? Where do you need fresh eyes to see God's perspective?

The Cross on the Side of the Road

One spring morning, I was heading to what I thought was going to be a momentous and emotionally heavy, but healing, conversation. I prayed in the car all the way, asking God to bring healing and truth into the conversation. I confessed that I trusted in Him, not the process I was engaging in.

Imagine my chagrin when, upon arriving at my destination, I found that the person with whom I was to have the conversation was out of town! We had clearly crossed our "icalendar" wires and I left feeling disappointed and empty. I was geared up. Emotionally charged. Ready for the "carefrontation" to occur.

But alas, it wasn't meant to be today.

Returning home, I asked God, "What's this about? What does it mean? Was I wrong to schedule this in the first place? Is this your way of telling me it was a bad idea to pursue it?" The combination of the emotional letdown, PMS creeping in, and the misty weather blurred my vision as I drove.

Then I saw the cross.

I mean a literal cross. On the side of the road.

It was the huge cross that a local church has in front of it and it was draped in a long white cloth that was dancing in the rainy breeze. Adorning the top was a crown of thorns.

It was a vivid reminder to me from God that THIS is where healing and redemption lie. Not in a conversation or a process or a life formula. The details of my situation were immediately dwarfed by the looming cross and its significance.

I began to pray for my friends whose lives were broken by their circumstances. For family members who weren't following God. For my own faith--that it would only and ever be based solely on the miraculous, redemptive work that was done on that cross.

It was a timely and necessary means to jog my memory and draw me into God's perspective on my circumstances. The truth is that everything else pales in comparison to the eternal truths that the cross represents. And Easter is a perfect time of year to be reminded of that each time I drive past a church with a liturgically dressed cross.

I am loved.

I am free from the burden of my past and of my failures.

I am part of God's family and I will spend eternity with Him.

Jesus died to pay a debt I could never pay to a holy God and HE IS ALIVE to intercede for me.

I ran the emotional gamut that morning, before I even hit lunchtime. But I also experienced my Savior's truth and perspective in a way that should last until we say, "Hosannah, Hosannah! Blessed is He who comes in the name of the LORD!" on Easter Sunday or when we get to Heaven.

Word Sparks

Conviction

Saturday morning in my jammies, drinking coffee, reading about Old Testament history and the sins and missteps of the tribes of Israel. One of those mornings I love to savor until the to-do list has to be taken care of.

I was tempted to keep reading in 1 Kings today because I hadn't read very far, when I remembered someone long ago suggesting that my time in Scripture should last until God stops me. He stopped me and had me scratching my head and searching my heart within just a couple of chapters today.

In 1 Kings 13 there is a man of God who comes to give King Jeroboam kind of a scary prophecy. The prophecy is not favorable to the king so he tells his guards to seize the man of God, and when he points at the culprit, his hand shrivels up. (Don't you love this stuff!?) "AAAHHH! Pray for me and heal my hand!" the king yells. (Wildly paraphrased by me)

He does. It heals. The king invites the man of God for dinner. (Again, not a word for word translation, you understand.)

"No can do," says the man. "You can offer me anything, but I've been told by God not to eat or drink anything on this mission. And I have to listen to God's instructions."

That was my first pause. What conviction, I thought. I will not be swayed by the king himself. I won't let power or influence or reward sway me from listening to and obeying what God has said. I want to be like that.

Read on.

The king sends a guy after him, who also invites him home to eat. And again, the man of God sticks to his guns and says he can't eat or drink on his mission from God. (Is this where Dan Aykroyd and John Belushi got their phrase?)

Never mind, says prophet #2. God told me you're supposed to come back with me and eat and drink with me at my house.

Word Sparks

Ok, says prophet #1. He goes back and eats at prophet #2's house, leaves and gets mauled and killed by a lion on the way home because he disobeyed. You just can't make this stuff up, I tell you.

Prophet #2 gets wind of the tragedy and says, "Yep. Look what happened because he didn't obey God. Poor guy. Let's bury him."

The story made me think about the strength of my convictions and where they come from. If the man of God in this story had strong enough conviction to say no to the king, what or who finally wore him down to a place of disobedience? And what was it like to feel that surge of conviction and God-confidence in the first place? Finally, how careful do I need to be when tossing out the words, "God told me..."?

I can tell you that I long for a deep sense of conviction that comes from God in my life. How glorious to have heard His voice so clearly that I can have an inner, resounding, "Yes!" from him to propel me in my daily actions and life's purpose. I also know that it doesn't take much for me to waver in that. To wonder if it really was God after all. To question the wisdom, convenience or timing of it all. Truth be known, I probably would have caved in front of the king.

But sometimes I feel so superior in my spirituality that I want to make others question their own convictions. It doesn't make sense to me, so I say, "Did God really say that to you?" Huh. That's what Satan said to Eve in the garden. Real spiritual...

So my takeaway is that I'm going to boldly ask God for conviction. To hear His voice. And for the inner fortitude, through the power of the Holy Spirit, not to be swayed.

And that I will have the grace and humility to trust that God is speaking to other people, too. And that Jesus died for them, too. And forgives them, too. It's not just about me. Ouch.

Lord, would you speak clearly to my heart and give me bold conviction to follow where you lead. Amen.

Read the whole story in 1 Kings 13. When have you

Word Sparks

heard God's direction clearly in your life? How have you responded? How would you like Him to change you?

Word Sparks

Toilets, Lies, and Humility

We bought a new house. Which was really an old house. We had a lot of work done: painting, two-sided fireplace put in, new shower in a bathroom, and various repairs that are too tedious to mention. All this happened before we moved in, so periodically (read: daily) I would go over to see the progress. One day I saw things coming together in a way that made me think we actually could live in this house.

While I was talking to my painter in the living room, he noticed that the carpet he was standing on was wet. We traced the source of water to an overflowing toilet on the other side of the wall, where the bathroom floor was a vast puddle and the water had found its way under the wall into the carpeted living room. Panic ensued.

After the water had been turned off, the mess cleaned up, and fans set up to dry the carpet, I left workers in place to continue progress on the rest of what needed to be done.

Later that day our family had a gathering of sorts

around some discrepancies in teen story-telling. (Read: lying) No matter what the infraction, I find that these issues are heart-breaking, and I've tried to explain to our son that when you lie to someone, it makes all the good in that relationship feel like manipulation, at worst, or questionable, at best.

So I cried a lot that day.

The next morning, as I continued my slow trek through Isaiah, praying for my son, and wondering if we've made a mistake with him, the house, or other things, I saw the blue highlighted words through the chapters that indicate qualities and names of God.

I was reminded that God is:

- The LORD my Maker
- Sovereign LORD
- My Redeemer
- The LORD Almighty
- The First and the Last
- A righteous God and Savior
- My King
- The Holy One

There may or may not be a lesson in or a reason for our suffering, as it were. A sin to confront. Character to build. Stories to share. But I do know that God wants to be found, He wants to be known, and He WILL be glorified.

I'm reminded that He loves me and is high and lifted up, seated on His throne, ruling the universe and my crazy little life. He sees my tears and hears my voice. And He transcends it all. And He says, *"I, even I, am he who comforts you."* (Isaiah 51:12)

Yes, and amen. *"Let him who walks in the dark, who has no light, trust in the name of the LORD and rely on his God."* (Isaiah 50:10)

Word Sparks

A Crown

A couple of years ago I spent two grueling hours in the dentist's chair to have a couple of crowns replaced, one of which was the right front tooth.

Back in fourth grade I hit this tooth on the bottom of the swimming pool while trying to show off for a friend and do a smiling back flip under water. (I know. Whatever you're thinking, my mom has probably brought to my attention.)

Anyway, I lived most of my adolescence with this slightly shorter front tooth to tide me over until I could get a "grown-up" crown. One day around 1990, I did just that.

And it was a fine tooth. Shiny porcelain that completed my smile as I met many new acquaintances. But over time my gums receded, revealing the black metal beneath the porcelain at the gum line, and I couldn't bleach it like the rest of my teeth, so it took on a slightly buttery shade. Considerably less attractive.

Word Sparks

So I was delighted to receive my new snowy white tooth to improve my smile.

Before I could see this beauty, however, the old crown had to be sawed in pieces by a diamond drill and cracked off my real tooth, which was lurking beneath the surface.

What did that look like?

Have you seen versions of Snow White's witch? That's pretty close.

A short, narrow, brown stump is what I have for a front tooth

In reality. It was horrifying. Like an Appalachian witchy woman, grinning over her cauldron at the entrance to her cave.

But that's my real tooth. This creamy white crown isn't me. It's the beautiful cover my dentist put there.

A crown I couldn't have applied myself.

A crown that covers a rotting (or so it appeared), shriveled stump that has become useless and appalling.

"That's good to remember, when I'm tempted to get

cocky about my beautiful smile!" I thought to myself, while admiring my new crown in the mirror that evening.

Then it occurred to me that this crown is just like what Jesus did for my sinful nature when He took my sin upon Himself on the cross.

He covered my sin with His spotless life. A beautiful crown, a white covering, a righteousness I did nothing to earn and couldn't possibly have provided for myself.

The prophet Isaiah said this:

"Come now, let us reason together,"
says the Lord.
"Though your sins are like scarlet,
they shall be as white as snow,
though they are red as crimson,
they shall be like wool. (Isaiah 1:18)

Our sin has been washed away by the perfect sacrifice of Christ. We did nothing to earn it. We can't do anything to keep it. So I can be comfortable revealing my weaknesses and my sin because we all have it! Why would I pretend this beauty that covers me is mine?!

Word Sparks

I have a brown stump for a tooth, and I'm not ashamed to admit it!

And I have a Savior who has washed away my sin and given me a righteousness I don't deserve.

My sins were as scarlet; now they're as white as snow!

Thanks be to God, through Jesus Christ!

Fear and Splendor

While beginning another trek through the prophet Isaiah one week, I took note of some powerful imagery in chapter 2. Now, I like the major prophets as much as the next gal, but sometimes the fire and brimstone imagery is a bit of a downer, I find.

This beginning section was no exception:

> *"Go into the rocks,*
> *hide in the ground*
> *from the dread of the LORD*
> *and the splendor of his majesty!"* (Isaiah 2:10)

The updated version of the NIV says, "*from the fearful presence of the LORD*", and the ESV calls it "*the terror of the LORD.*"

I couldn't help but wonder who these unfortunate people are who have to fear and hide from God. The heading of Isaiah 2:6-22 is "*The Day of the LORD,*" which usually describes something pretty dramatic, if I understand a lot of the Bible right. But the stunning thing about this verse wasn't the specific dramatic imagery here as much as it was the *exact* repetition of the phrase again in verses 19 and 21. I wrote in the margin of verse 2, "You can't handle the power and beauty of God!" and I still think that's the case. Let's call that the Holy Spirit's primary revelation to me that morning. God is too much for mere mortals to comprehend.

When I read the rest of chapter 2 and saw those aspects of fear and hiding repeated, God's Spirit started to reveal something else to me. Descriptions of those who are going to have to hide and fear the presence of the LORD are sprinkled throughout this chapter. They are "the proud and lofty." and those who "bow down to the work of their hands, to what their fingers have made." Umm... that's me, if I'm being completely honest.

And other places in Scripture point to the fact that there will be those who experience God's wrath during the day of the LORD, at some point in the future. But I didn't feel threatened or afraid, despite my acute awareness of these shortcomings.

I relate to the places in Scripture that talk about

longing to come into God's Presence, not running away from it. The spots that elicit joy and comfort in being with God, protected and loved. What's the difference?

This is when I had my epiphany.

I wrote in the margin after verse 21: "I want to stand in confident awe in your presence, Lord. To experience the dread of the Lord and the splendor of your majesty." I know my sin and that I'm not at all worthy to stand in God's presence on my own. But I read these verses and they are, in my life, inextricably linked with these:

"Therefore, brothers, since we have confidence to enter the Most Holy Place by the blood of Jesus, by a new and living way opened for us through the curtain that is, his body, and since we have a great priest over the house of God, let us draw near to God with a sincere heart in full assurance of faith, having our hearts sprinkled to cleanse us from a guilty conscience and having our bodies washed with pure water." (Hebrews 10:19-21)

I can run *to* God and not *from* the terror of His

presence because of Jesus!

I can "approach the throne of grace with confidence" (Heb. 4:16) because Jesus paid the price for my sin and took God's wrath from me onto Himself. I can draw near to God--not run from Him--because the blood of Jesus sprinkled our hearts and cleansed us from ALL unrighteousness, so we can have full assurance of faith, based on HIS work and righteousness, not our own.

I can experience a balance of assurance and awe. Freedom and fear.

Author Francis Chan says, "...when we love God, we naturally run to Him--frequently and zealously."

I heard an author talk about our only refuge from God being in God. And I think the combination of these ideas, albeit somewhat counterintuitive, is right. Yes, a parent will discipline a child he loves and the child wants to run away from the discipline when he's disobeyed. But there is also great joy and safety in knowing that same parent will protect the child and provide for him with all his energy out of fierce love.

Word Sparks

It is a dreadful thing to fall into the hands of the living God, says the author of Hebrews (10:31). Thanks be to God for Jesus Christ, who made a way for us to stand in His presence in full assurance of faith because of His great love and sacrifice. He has redeemed us from God's wrath and brought us into His family as sons and heirs.

Word Sparks

Whose Honor?

When my son was a young teenager I read *The Five Love Languages of Teenagers* by Gary Chapman, which I highly recommend when your kids are about eleven. As I pondered how to best fill my teen's love tank, I also had a couple of interesting and challenging conversations with folks about parenting. It seems the best we can do for our children at any age is pray and love them toward the most solid foundation of God-confidence possible. Not to modify their behavior or spare them any pain in life--that's how we learn, after all--but to train them to lean on God and depend on Him only for their sense of self and security.

In the Bible there is a story of a man whose parents either didn't have this goal or whose heart was just too hard to be molded. His appetite for man's praise and power was insatiable. Here's just one example of the warped perspective Haman lived with:

"Calling together his friends and Zeresh, his wife, Haman boasted to them about his vast wealth, his many

sons, and all the ways the king had honored him and how he had elevated him above the other nobles and officials. 'And that's not all,' Haman added. 'I'm the only person Queen Esther invited to accompany the king to the banquet she gave. And she has invited me along with the king tomorrow. But all this gives me no satisfaction as long as I see that Jew Mordecai sitting at the king's gate.'" (Esther 5:10-13)

Even though the king had honored Haman, he had a fertile family, and everyone in the kingdom recognized his power and accomplishment, "that Jew Mordecai sitting at the gate," who wouldn't bow down to him, overshadowed everything good in his life.

It got me thinking: whose honor do I care about most? Where does my sense of well-being come from? Who do I strive to please in my daily activities?

The Bible tells me that the answer to all these questions should be God, of course. But is that how I live it out when I worry more about a friend being mad at me than being obedient? Is that the reality when I set professional or personal goals without consulting God or considering His perspective? Am I living for God's honor alone when I choose to lie? When my insecurities drive me to treat others poorly? When gratitude for all of God's blessings are minimized and I focus on the few things I want that I don't have? What about when I fall prey to the green monster of envy over someone else's good looks, good fortune, or good life?

These behaviors and attitudes all reflect a Haman-esque perspective. A focus on self and a pride that keeps me from experiencing God's best in my life and peace in His presence. And when I recognize the symptoms, the only remedy is to repent.

You see, I want my son to have a strong sense of identity in Christ, but I want it for myself, too! I want to focus like a laser beam on the things of God: what pleases Him, what is holy, serving others. But I'm incapable of that kind of life without the powerful intervention of the Holy Spirit and the redeeming work of Christ's perfect sacrifice on the cross.

Word Sparks

Thanks be to God that we have access to these because of the grace and love of God our Father! He speaks ALL the love languages, because He is love. What better place to turn in order to be transformed!

Conversations

So I met a guy in a bar last night.

I was meeting a couple of friends who used to work for my husband, and when we meet, we meet at the restaurant my husband used to own, which is where they used to work. As we were catching up on jobs, relationships, and the state of politics and the economy, a man seated a few barstools away from us joined our conversation.

First, he commented on the frustrations of the aging process. Brother, I hear you there! We nodded politely, then turned back to our conversation.

After he'd had a couple more drinks and our conversation seemed more interesting to him, he chimed in again. This time he had overheard us talking about gay marriage laws and differing views of Christians. My friends and I have agreed to disagree on many issues, this being one of them. Our new friend directed his comment to me when he said, "so you're one of those judgmental Christians who thinks all gay people will go to hell."

Awesome.

I responded that if by judgmental he meant putting myself in a superior position to others, then, no. I'm not judgmental. (This after he wondered why I just didn't embrace my judgmentalism.)

"Do you believe there's a hell?"

"Yes," I replied.

"Do you believe people will actually go there?"

"Yes."

"Do you believe all gay people will go to hell?"

"Absolutely not."

His eyebrows raised, he pursed his lips and nodded slowly, as if to say, "Tell me more." So I did.

As my friends had quickly exited for a cigarette, throwing me under the bus to engage our new friend alone, I continued:

"You see, I don't think it's what anybody *does* that determines whether or not they go to heaven. It's who they know. If someone knows Jesus and accepts what HE did by dying on the cross for them, that's what determines whether or not they go to heaven."

More nodding.

Then, after some talk of Americans not knowing the difference between consubstantiation and transubstantiation, and illiterate spirituality, and "slaughtering" religious differences, we discovered that the barstool denizen was, in fact, Canadian. He'd been living here for ten years and had assessed the American spiritual zeitgeist so thoroughly that there really was nothing left to discuss.

So he finished his meal, paid his tab, and left.

My friends and I debriefed.

Turns out they really agree with a lot that he was saying. But he was such a jerk about it that they didn't trust themselves to engage calmly in my defense as he ranted about "literalist Christians" and their problems interpreting the first two chapters of Genesis (idiots!). There was some awkward head-shaking and sighing before we moved on to the next topic in his absence.

The following morning I replayed the conversations

in my head. Did I represent Christ well? Did I speak truth? How can I keep engaging people on issues like biblical interpretations of social issues without appearing to be (or actually being) ignorant or condescending or rude?

Thank God for the power of the Holy Spirit! I was leaning heavily on His direction that night, for sure. And so, the next morning, I was able to release my second-guessing and hand-wringing to His sovereignty. May my Canadian spiritual nemesis find truth and peace in other conversations as God reveals Himself more and more.

He is Risen!

Easter Sunday.

What better opportunity for teenage boys to ride, jump with, and fall off bikes? One Easter weekend we travelled over the river and through the woods--to Grandmother's house we went. There, we found skate parks and piles of dirt to make a young boy's heart pound and adrenaline race through his veins.

A few crashes? Not to worry. Our chiropractor will soon put everything back in order.

The beauty of the huge mounds of dirt on the neighbor's property was the height to which bikers could soar if they had enough momentum. Some went higher than others, of course, but everyone involved caught some air.

The freedom and joy in the faces of the bikers this weekend was more than apt for Resurrection Sunday. As I contemplate all that Easter means for us, I am more and more in awe of the perfect plan and effect God's sovereign power wrought.

Word Sparks

As we embrace the glory of the cross--the ultimate victory over all the sin that weighs me down and the death that threatened to separate us from God forever-- we have access to God's Holy Spirit, who will empower and transform us to live in freedom with God.

Because He is risen.

Death could not hold Him. The grave could not keep Him from rising again.

And because of that glorious sacrifice and victory, I am free to soar. I'm free to live without the burden of my past. I can run unhindered by sin that trips me up and makes me stumble.

Because He is risen.

I want my life in Christ to be like the bikers who caught the most air last weekend: exuberant, free, and exhilarating. Defying gravity and moving forward in power. We can live like this!

Because He is risen!

Evil

One night during the Seattle International Film Festival, I went to see a French film with a friend. It was called *The Clink of Ice*. The premise was fascinating. A writer named Charles has cancer and lives alone in an isolated house with his housekeeper (and his young Russian lover for a while, but that's incidental). His wife and son have left him and he drinks wine all day long. One day a man comes to the house and introduces himself as his cancer. The movie then follows Charles as his relationship with the incarnation of his cancer evolves and forces him to reevaluate many aspects of his life. It's not pretty.

Eventually, the housekeeper also develops cancer and so the house now has a dynamic of four instead of two. Charles and Louisa (the housekeeper). Charles and his cancer. Louisa and her cancer. And brain cancer with breast cancer.

What has stuck with me since I saw the movie were lines that Charles' cancer kept repeating: Evil always wins. Evil will always be here. His message seemed to be that no matter how many regrets you have in life--no matter how much more time you'd like to have to live your dreams and make things right--cancer doesn't care. It is, in fact, one of life's great equalizers.

And the following week, as part of my family and I sat in on the trial for my sister-in-law's murderer, I went back to the lines of the movie and wondered: is it true?

Does evil win? What do we do with the apparent injustice and depravity all around us?

Are we powerless against the forces of evil in this world? It's scary and disgusting out there.

Where is God when tragedy strikes?

I am happy to report that, even through my tears, God's truth penetrated my doubt. The truth of Scripture and the resonant truth of experience. Here are a few examples of what the Bible says about this:

"...the one who is in you is greater than the one who is in the world." (1 John 4:4)

"It is mine to avenge; I will repay...There is no god besides me. I put to death and I bring to life, I have

wounded and I will heal, and no one can deliver out of my hand." (Deuteronomy 32:35, 39)

"Peace I leave with you; my peace I give you. I do not give to you as the world gives. Do not let your hearts be troubled and do not be afraid." (John 4:27)

"Finally, be strong in the Lord and in his mighty power. Put on the full armor of God, so that you can take your stand against the devil's schemes. For our struggle is not against flesh and blood, but against the rulers, against the authorities, against the powers of this dark world and against the spiritual forces of evil in the heavenly realms. Therefore put on the full armor of God, so that when the day of evil comes, you may be able to stand your ground, and after you have done everything, to stand." (Ephesians 6:10-13)

"His divine power has given us everything we need for life and godliness through our knowledge of him who

called us by his own glory and goodness. Through these he has given us his very great and precious promises so that through them you may participate in the divine nature and escape the corruption of the world by evil desires." (2 Peter 1:3-4)

"...If God is for us, who can be against us? He who did not spare his own Son, but gave him up for us all--how will he not also, along with him, graciously give us all things?...For I am convinced that neither death nor life, neither angels nor demons, neither the present nor the future, nor any powers, neither height nor depth, nor anything else in all creation, will be able to separate us from the love of God that is in Christ Jesus our Lord." (Romans 8:31-32, 38-39)

"Hallelujah! Salvation and glory and power belong to our God, for true and just are his judgments." (Revelation 19:1-2)

Word Sparks

"...and hope does not disappoint us..." (Romans 5:5)

And there's much, much more. Our God is sovereign and victorious over evil. Read the book of Revelation. He wins, my friends. He wins. Even when the darkness seems profound, He is there, comforting and working out the details of our lives to bring Him glory and make us into the image of Christ.

As for experience, I know that my Redeemer lives because His Spirit is alive and active in me every day. I sense His promptings, His conviction, His inexplicable peace, and His assurance that He will never leave me or forsake me. I am a stronger, more loving person than I am capable of being. He holds me together when I would fall apart on my own. He loves me completely and holds me when I feel utterly alone. He's done it countless times in the past week alone.

Evil most certainly does not win.

Our Lord God Almighty reigns. And He has already won the victory. We just haven't seen all the acts of the play yet.

Word Sparks

Yes, evil will always be here with us while we live on this earth. But when we have a relationship with the God of the universe through Jesus, we are more than victorious over the evil. He is our peace. He is our comfort. He is our advocate.

Cancer will never have the last word over an empty grave. Jesus already beat death and sin.

They just don't know it yet.

Dilemma

Many mornings I'll open my Bible to where I last left off and determine that I will read until God stops me. Sometimes that turns into reading until somebody in the house wakes up. Sometimes it turns into reading until my coffee is cold. And sometimes it turns into reading until my stomach starts growling. I consider all of those things to fall under the category of "until God stops me."

One morning, I sat in my customary Bible-reading chair, coffee cup warm and good intentions in hand. I read exactly four verses when God really did stop me. This was the passage:

"What do you think? If a man owns a hundred sheep, and one of them wanders away, will he not leave the ninety-nine on the hills and go to look for the one that wandered off? And if he finds it, truly I tell you, he is happier about that one sheep than about the ninety-nine that did not wander off. In the same way your Father in heaven is not willing that any of these little ones should perish." (Matthew 18:12-14)

Word Sparks

At an earlier reading of this passage I had written in the margin: "How can I make God happy as one of the ninety-nine?" And my thoughts went immediately to the story of the prodigal son and his older, somewhat cantankerous brother. Read the finale of that story and see if you notice a connection between the two:

"Meanwhile, the older son was in the field. When he came near the house, he heard music and dancing. So he called one of the servants and asked him what was going on. 'Your brother has come,' he replied, 'and your father has killed the fattened calf because he has him back safe and sound.'

"The older brother became angry and refused to go in. So his father went out and pleaded with him. But he answered his father, 'Look! All these years I've been slaving for you and never disobeyed your orders. Yet you never gave me even a young goat so I could celebrate with my friends. But when this son of yours who has squandered your property with prostitutes comes home, you kill the fattened calf for him!'

"'My son,' the father said, 'you are always with me, and everything I have is yours. But we had to celebrate and be glad, because this brother of yours was dead and is alive again; he was lost and is found.'" (Luke 15:25-32)

I've always related to the older brother in this parable and to the sheep that didn't wander. I don't have a dramatic or scandalous past that evokes gasps and wide eyes as I recount it. But as I contemplated how to make God happy as an obedient child who doesn't wander off in wicked escapades, He revealed to me this sobering thought:

I was lost and I still wander.

There was a time when I was outside God's family. When I was, as Colossians and Ephesians describe so clearly, an enemy of God, an object of wrath, alone, without hope or God in the world.

He brought me near through the sacrificial death of Jesus. And that was when God rejoiced over me coming into His family. That's when I came back into the family I was created to be a part of.

Then God reminded me (as He has been trying to teach me this over and over again recently) that I still wander. I still follow the wicked inclinations of my heart by putting myself and my comfort above the needs of others. By leaving the intentional time in God's presence to pursue useless and fruitless activities. By tilling the soil of my soul for seeds of resentment and bitterness and judgment against the people in my life. Oh, I still wander alright. And every time I come back, He is happy! Do you know why God is happy when we come back to Him?

Because He wants us near Him!

He created us for profound, intimate, continual, and eternal relationship with Him and it breaks His heart when we stray. So I can make God happy as one of the ninety-nine sheep by staying close to Him. And by investing in the lives of those who are not. That's the beauty of community.

The chief end of man is to glorify God and enjoy Him forever. Or as John Piper says, to glorify God *by enjoying*

Him forever. There is satisfaction and joy for us and for God when we are close.

So when I wander and the Holy Spirit convicts me of it, all that's necessary is a repentant heart. Then the forgiveness Jesus purchased for me on the cross propels me back into the arms of the Good Shepherd. Once again, one of the ninety-nine. Close to the Father. As I was meant to be.

Word Sparks

Invitations

Don't you love getting an invitation? Parties, graduations, weddings, retirements. It's an honor to be invited somewhere. And it feels good to know that our presence is requested. Someone wants to share an event with us, whether it's a celebration or a remembrance. But sometimes an invitation has implications beneath the surface and sometimes we bring our own bias. We may wonder who else is invited? What will I wear? Will there be food? What if so-and-so is there? Awkward... But overall, an invitation that comes is usually a pleasant surprise.

Hollywood is known for its glamour and spectacular parties. The *Vanity Fair* Oscar Party is arguably the most coveted invitation of the year, costing the host over one million dollars to put on. The reason for all this hoopla is simple: **the harder the party is to get into, the more people will clamor to be invited**.

We receive all kinds of invitations: graduations, weddings, retirement, birthday parties. Do you think there's a difference in being invited to The *Vanity Fair* Oscar Party and Lily's Strawberry Shortcake third birthday party? Um, yeah. Whether we want to admit it or not, the importance and/or rarity of the event will have great influence on our response.

There are other kinds of invitations in life, too, aren't there? Isn't a marriage proposal a kind of invitation--an invitation from a man to a woman to share his name and a life together? A casual invitation to coffee or lunch can mean a lot to a lonely person. *Ultimately an invitation is about relationship.* Whether the event is to celebrate relationships--like a wedding--or just including people by being together, marking milestones in life is better when it can be shared in the context of relationship.

What kinds of invitations does God proffer in our lives? Here are three examples:

1. Seek Me. Because God places such importance on relationships, one of His primary invitations to His people throughout the Bible is to seek Him. And His promise is that we will find Him. When the Israelites had been disobedient and God allowed the Chaldeans (Babylonians) to take them as exiles and prisoners into a foreign land, He sent this encouraging invitation through the prophet Jeremiah to the confused, distraught people: *This is what the LORD says: "When seventy years are completed for Babylon, I will come to you and fulfill my gracious promise to bring you back to this place. 11 For I know the plans I have for you," declares the LORD, "plans to prosper you and not to harm you, plans to give you hope and a future. 12 Then you will call upon me and come and pray to me, and I will listen to you. 13 You will seek me and find me when you seek me with all your heart. 14 I will be found by you," declares the LORD, "and will bring you back from captivity. I will gather you from all the nations and places where I have banished you," declares the LORD, "and will bring you back to the place from which I carried you into exile."* (Jeremiah 29:10-14) He gave the same invitation through the prophet Amos earlier when He said: *4 This is what the LORD says to the house of Israel:* **"Seek me and live***; 5 do not seek Bethel, ⬚do not go to*

Gilgal, do not journey to Beersheba. ⬚For Gilgal will surely go into exile, and Bethel will be reduced to nothing." ⬚6 **Seek the LORD and live,** *or he will sweep through the house of Joseph like a fire; it will devour, and Bethel will have no one to quench it.* (Amos 5:4-6) In both cases, to two different groups of people, God issues the same invitation that He offers to us: *Come and seek me.* He wants to be found because He wants to have relationship with us. Jesus also issued this invitation to those who would follow Him when He said: *"Ask and it will be given to you; seek and you will find; knock and the door will be opened to you. For everyone who asks receives; he who seeks finds; and to him who knocks, the door will be opened.* (Matthew 7:7-8) It's a little like a game of hide and seek with a small child who calls out from his hiding place in the closet, "I'm in here!" making it easy to find Him. That's our God: He longs to be found and known and He invites us over and over to look for Him so He can have relationship with us.

2. Rest In Me. Jesus offers this invitation in the

gospel of Matthew: *28 "Come to me, all you who are weary and burdened, and I will give you rest. 29 Take my yoke upon you and learn from me, for I am gentle and humble in heart, and you will find rest for your souls. 30 For my yoke is easy and my burden is light."* (Matthew 11:28-30) Doesn't that sound nice? Rest for your soul. Who doesn't get soul weary from time to time? Who doesn't feel the burden of life when the pressure mounts and the deadlines are looming large? When relationships are tense and we feel inadequate for the tasks ahead of us? Jesus gives us the invitation to come to Him with all of that. To exchange the self-propelled efforts to manage our lives for the total surrender of our wills to His ways. The reason that Jesus' yoke is easy and His burden is light is because He's already done everything necessary for us to walk in obedience and joy. 2 Peter 1:3-4 says this: *3 His divine power has given us everything we need for life and godliness through our knowledge of him who called us by his own glory and goodness. 4 Through these he has given us his very great and precious promises, so that through them you may participate in the divine nature and escape the corruption in the world caused by evil desires.* In other words, Jesus has done everything necessary for us to live lives as we were created to live them through His obedient, perfect sacrifice on the cross! Our efforts to just improve ourselves instead of allow Him to transform us are what causes so much of our frustrations. Truth be known, many of us are carrying burdens in life that God never asked us to carry and He wants us to give them to Him. Then we can experience "soul rest."

3. Follow Me. This invitation may be the hardest to swallow--and certainly the hardest to fully accept. *[23]And he said to all, "If anyone would come after me, let him deny himself and take up his cross daily and follow me. [24]For whoever would save his life will lose it, but whoever loses his life for my sake will save it. [25] For what does it profit a man if he gains the whole world and loses or forfeits himself? [26]For whoever is ashamed of me and of my words, of him will the Son of Man be ashamed when he comes in his glory and the glory of the Father and of the holy* *angels.*" (Luke 9:23-26) This invitation seems to be filled with paradoxes. As if an invite to a birthday party came in the mail and said, "if you'd like to keep your coat, then give it away at the door." But if I'm going to a party and can't trust that I'll remember where my coat is, the best thing to do is to trust it to the person at the coat check so it'll be safe and waiting for me at the end of the night. And the logic of this cross analogy has to do with the ancient tradition of taking up a cross. When a condemned man was going to be crucified under Roman rule in the time of the disciples, he was required to carry the beam of the cross to the place of execution. Jesus and his disciples would have seen this happen and Jesus Himself was going to carry the beam of HIS cross to Golgotha. It symbolizes the fact that we are to consider ourselves dead to our former way of life and should live as if that's true. We are no longer slaves to sin, but Christ has bought our freedom through His trip to the cross and resurrection, so we live for Him now. (Galatians 2:20 "*I have been crucified with Christ. It is no longer I who live, but Christ who lives in me. And the life I now live in the flesh I live by faith in the Son of God, who loved me and gave himself for me.*") This invitation refers to a complete transfer of allegiance. I no longer live for myself; I'm to deny myself. That is the natural, carnal urges that used to have power over me. When I let go of my life I receive the life God has for me. The one I was created to live. That's what He's inviting us to. As C.S. Lewis says in *Mere Christianity*, "...mere improvement is not redemption." Jesus did not die and rise from the grave to make us better versions of our former selves. He died to redeem us from our old life--to buy us back from a life of slavery to sin and death so we could be new creations, becoming more and more like Him in the process of sanctification.

So what kind of invitations have you received from God recently? What are you sensing that He may be inviting you? Is He inviting you to just look for Him to see if He's real? Is He inviting you to lay down some burdens that have been too much? Or are you receiving a more challenging invitation? My challenge to you is to be still

Word Sparks

and ask God to reveal the kind of invitation He has for you. You may want to write down what you hear God say. Just be sure to RSVP.

Word Sparks

Battling Sloth

Many of us have heard lessons on the story of Mary and Martha when Jesus comes to dine at their house, and most people I know relate to Martha. She's the busy one. The one who resented her sister sitting at Jesus' feet and listening, nobly, to His teaching while she slaved over a meal for guests. "Martha, Martha," the Lord chides her affectionately. "Get over it," He seems to say. Not really, but you know. Martha's busy, but Mary is *with Jesus*. Being with Jesus is what matters, so don't get your knickers in a twist about the dirty dishes.

I don't get it.

I've never been a Martha. Never wanted to be. I've never been accused of being too busy or avoiding social settings by bussing tables or doing dishes. Nope. I want to sit down, be comfortable, eating and drinking and making merry, thank you very much. I used to think that I, like Mary, had chosen the one important thing: sitting. But, you see, that wasn't Jesus' point at all.

I've come to realize recently that I've been using my

pride to disguise my sloth as "mary-ness." I've spent considerable time thinking that I'm rather spiritual in my pursuits and that I should let the less erudite among us take up the serving slack while I illuminate Scripture and enlighten the masses. Could you refill my coffee, please, while you're at it?

Nice.

But you know what God has shown me?

Laziness is a sin.

My laziness comes from a deep-seated selfishness and a potent priority for my own comfort. Not from a desire for fellowship and a hunger for God's truth to be revealed. It is counterintuitive to my nature to serve others. And there's nothing in that to take pride in, believe me.

But there is hope for me, my friends.

One weekend I visited my brother-in-law and sister-in-law in New Jersey. My husband's parents were there, as well. Over the course of the weeks leading up to my trip, I had been repeating a mantra to myself that I continued on the other side of the country: "Don't be lazy. Don't be lazy." Like a highly hormonal teenager fights lust, or the way an alcoholic fights the temptation to drink, I've been leaning into God for the strength to *not* give into my slothful tendencies so He can develop mature character in me.

That weekend He revealed plenty of opportunities for me to serve. And He revealed lots of times I was tempted to make a decision based on what was best for me. It felt like a sort of tug-of-war inside me. But what I discovered when I was honest about my desires and confessed my selfishness over and over was that His Spirit prompted me to do the dishes. Or hold the baby. Or unload groceries. Or pour a glass of milk. Or make some coffee. Gestures that never would have occurred to me on my own were revealed as an opportunity to trust God to make me into the kind of woman He wants me to be. And most exciting of all--there was joy and satisfaction in it!

So while I was dismayed by the realization that I am,

in fact, slothful and selfish by nature, I also realized that God loves me anyway and wants to change me. Thanks be to God! I can't do that myself. If left to my own devices, I will always choose my own comfort and ease. My comfort is my idol. And God wants to change that. As discouraging as it is initially to name my sin and see it for what it is, it's equally *encouraging* to see God working in me, through the transforming power of the Holy Spirit, to eradicate my old nature and replace it with His.

And I want to change. I want it desperately. So I will choose to serve others and walk into the life He has for me by obedience. And I will trust Him to do what only He can do in my life to make me into the person He created me to be when He knit me together in my mother's womb. And when I fail, I will call it what it is. Sloth. Selfishness. Pride. And I will be reminded that it is only by God's grace that I can call Him Abba, Father. I'm not such a great prize, but He is. And He has redeemed even my most despicable moments and moods for His glory.

Diagnosis or Cure?

When I was about 45 years old I had the auspicious pleasure of hearing my doctor inform me that I had an ear infection. Do adults even get those?! I remember holding my son in my arms as a toddler after the surgeon had put tubes in his ears for the countless ear infections he had had, but I always thought that it was an affliction one outgrew.

Apparently not.

Thankfully, I left the doctor's office with new knowledge and a prescription for Z-Pak, my new favorite antibiotic cocktail. Ear pain gone; life back to normal. Diagnosis and cure in one fell swoop.

In the Old Testament book of Leviticus, God outlines the priestly duties for Aaron and his sons, who are not only intermediaries for God's people in sin atonement, but are also instructed to carry out butcher duties for the sacrificial animals and provide extensive diagnoses of diseases, like a community doctor. Priest, butcher and doctor are not what I would consider complementary professions, but there you have it in Scripture. Take a look at just a few examples of the medical knowledge necessary for Aaron and his sons to perform their God-given duties:

8The priest is to examine him, and if the rash has spread in the skin, he shall pronounce him unclean; it is an infectious disease.

9 "When anyone has an infectious skin disease, he must be brought to the priest. 10 The priest is to examine him, and if there is a white swelling in the skin that has turned the hair white and if there is raw flesh in the swelling, 11 it is a chronic skin disease and the priest shall pronounce him unclean. He is not to put him in isolation, because he is already unclean. (Leviticus 13:8-11)

18 "When someone has a boil on his skin and it heals, 19and in the place where the boil was, a white swelling or reddish-white spot appears, he must present himself to the priest. 20 The priest is to examine it, and if it appears to be more than skin deep and the hair in it has turned white, the priest shall pronounce him unclean. It is an infectious

Word Sparks

skin disease that has broken out where the boil was. (Leviticus 13:18-20)

24 "When someone has a burn on his skin and a reddish-white or white spot appears in the raw flesh of the burn, 25the priest is to examine the spot, and if the hair in it has turned white, and it appears to be more than skin deep, it is an infectious disease that has broken out in the burn. The priest shall pronounce him unclean; it is an infectious skin disease. (Leviticus 13:24-25)

The priest shall pronounce him unclean. Yep. You're sick alright. Now get outta town. That was the pronouncement. Then come back in a week and we'll see if you're better or worse. Would any of us keep going to a doctor like that?!

A few chapters later we see that the priests have a formula for pronouncing the formerly diseased person clean. Like with animal food choices earlier in the book, God has carefully outlined preemptive regulations to keep His children healthy. He has designated some animals clean and some animals unclean. Certain animals are pronounced "unclean" because of how they digest food or where they live. Kosher guidelines, like all other parts of God's law, were designed to protect God's people. In the same way, after a skin disease has gone away, the priests have guidelines for pronouncing that person clean--able to rejoin society and come back into God's presence.

But there's no cure.

God outlines a formula to prevent disease. He gives extensive information to the priests for diagnosing disease. But He alone is the Healer.

Enter Jesus.

Those with skin diseases, fevers, blood disorders, evil spirits, blindness, paralysis, shriveled limbs, and dropsy (Dr. Luke liked to make sure we knew the details of the disease.) came to Jesus for healing. Sometimes He went to them instead. Either way, He looked at the "unclean" affliction that had been pronounced and reached out in compassion, with healing. Other biblical characters had brought people back to life occasionally.

And in the book of Acts we see the disciples performing all kinds of inexplicable events. Miracles aren't unique to the gospels. But Jesus was different because He completely obliterated the line between clean and unclean by bringing absolute healing in body, mind and spirit.

The law forbidding an unclean person the human contact we all need didn't apply to Jesus because as God Himself, His absolute holiness couldn't be compromised. So Jesus could touch those who were isolated when He healed them, thereby giving them acceptance as well as health.

4 Surely he took up our infirmities
and carried our sorrows,
yet we considered him stricken by God,
smitten by him, and afflicted.
5 But he was pierced for our transgressions,
he was crushed for our iniquities;
the punishment that brought us peace was upon him,
and by his wounds we are healed.
6 We all, like sheep, have gone astray,
each of us has turned to his own way;
and the LORD has laid on him

the iniquity of us all. (Isaiah 53:4-6)

These words of the prophet Isaiah refer to Jesus, our Healer. Look at what the apostle Peter wrote about Jesus hundreds of years later:

23 When they hurled their insults at him, he did not retaliate; when he suffered, he made no threats. Instead, he entrusted himself to him who judges justly. 24 He himself bore our sins in his body on the tree, so that we might die to sins and live for righteousness; by his wounds you have been healed. 25 For you were like sheep going astray, but now you have returned to the Shepherd and Overseer of your souls. (1 Peter 2:23-25)

We have been healed by Jesus once and for all! The implications of this piece of history and theology are astounding!

We are no longer slaves to sin.

We are freed from the penalty of our sinful nature because of Christ's sacrifice.

We are forgiven.

Word Sparks

We are redeemed--we have been bought from darkness and brought into light.

Our eternal destiny is secure in Heaven.

We belong to God.

Thanks be to God! Whether we have been physically healed of disease or affliction, or we've been freed from emotional brokenness or addiction, God is the ultimate Healer. Even those of us who are still suffering from the very things we beg God to take away can find solace in the fact that we don't have to live under the weight of the suffering. Our healing--in the most profound sense of the word--has already taken place when we put our trust in Jesus' death and resurrection. And that perspective can be liberating if we let it sink in.

The Holy Spirit's power is limitless and sovereign. When we submit ourselves to His guidance and ask God to reveal His perspective on our lives, we can see beyond physical or emotional limitations to the boundless glory of the freedom of our souls.

[8]We are hard pressed on every side, but not crushed;

perplexed, but not in despair; [9]persecuted, but not abandoned; struck down, but not destroyed... (2 Corinthians 4:8-9)

Yes, we may suffer, but we have already been healed.

If sin is the incurable disease whose diagnosis was made at Adam and Eve's first bite of fruit, then we can rejoice in the cure: Jesus' perfect life and sacrifice to raise us up with Him in glorious resurrection.

By His wounds we have been healed. Amen.

"Your Majesty"

Years ago, as I was involved in a Bible study that focused on God's holiness, I found that there were examples of the concepts I was learning everywhere. Does that happen to you, too? I was seeing God's holiness all day long! We also had discussions about how to reconcile God's "otherness"--the separation of His holy character from ours--with the intimate knowledge and love He has for His children.

Is He to be feared or loved?

Can one do both?

How are we to approach this mighty and loving God and Father?

During that time my husband and I went to see *The King's Speech* with Colin Firth and Geoffrey Rush. And in it there is one particular scene that has clarified this dichotomy for me in a powerful way.

Moments after King George VI has gone through the ceremonial Accession Council, wearing his full royal regalia, he greets his wife and daughters, who are playing in a hallway. There is a pregnant pause with significant looks communicating deep emotion between spouses who are now king and queen of the nation.

Then King George looks down at his daughters, who stop playing to look at him. The older sister, Elizabeth, leans toward her younger sister and whispers, "Curtsy." Both girls formally take hold of their identical dresses, nod their heads as they curtsy, and pronounce quietly and solemnly, "Your majesty."

With only slight hesitation, the king takes both girls in his arms and kisses them affectionately on the forehead, thereby firmly establishing his role as father as well as king.

This is our God!

He is high and lifted up. Sovereign on His throne in heaven as the angels sing, "Holy, holy, holy is the Lord, God Almighty. The earth is full of His glory!"

AND....

He searches and knows the depths of our hearts and minds for He created us in our mother's womb.

Word Sparks

Our response to seeing Him in His holiness is to fall on our faces before such power and majesty.

His response is to accept our worship--for He alone is worthy--and to lift us up and love us as a Father loves His children.

He is my King.

He is my Father.

Thanks be to God!

Word Sparks

Candy Hoarder

I had a rather unattractive character flaw revealed to me after Christmas one year.

After dinner one night, my husband was rooting around in what we call the "snack drawer." It's where we used to keep our stash of Oreos and Cheez-Its, etc. It's the drawer all my teenage son's friends used to gravitate toward when they came over--especially the ones with conscientious parents who wouldn't buy those things. I corrupted them.

Anyway, he found the candy I had put there from my Christmas stocking. Reese's cups, Butterfingers, Twix, and Snickers. Yum. Per my very specific request, they had been dropped off by Santa on Christmas Eve, and once the Christmas decor had been put away, I put the contents of my stocking in the snack drawer.

When my husband discovered them, he asked who wanted which candy for dessert.

"Uhhh...That's *my* stocking candy," I pointed out.

"All of this?" he asked, as if he didn't remember buying it and placing it in my stocking himself.

"Yeah. MY candy."

"Ok. I'll have Oreos," he replied.

Later, when I noticed his mood had changed considerably, I asked him if he was mad that I wouldn't share my candy. His response?

"I just can't believe how quickly such nastiness comes out of your mouth."

Ouch.

A short time later God spoke as clearly to me as He has ever done, telling me that the candy was like the gifts He gives to me. They're from Him (like the candy was from Tony) and in my selfishness, I don't want to share. I couldn't believe it! Tony went to work and earned the money and went to the store and bought the candy and put it in my stocking. And I claimed it as MINE? Really?

In what ways do I do that with what God's given me? With my possessions? With my time? With my talents? Everything I have is from Him! It should inspire me to

Word Sparks

give generously and to lay all my plans before my Father and hold all things loosely.

But I don't.

So I repented in tears on the edge of our tub and then went to the drawer to get the Twix bars that were there, which are my husband's favorite. I placed them under the pillow on his side of the bed with a note that said, "I'm sorry. Will U 4-give me?"

When he discovered them that night, he laughed and took me in his arms and said that, yes, he would forgive me.

That's grace.

Word Sparks

Fully Equipped

When we used to live on a fairly steep incline and my son and his friends liked to snowboard and mountain bike, my creamy sedan was just not cutting it, so we traded it in for something more practical. Wet, muddy teenage boys were then welcome in my all-wheel drive vehicle.

As we shopped for cars, we were intrigued by the many features that were available for safety and comfort. Air bags are now standard. Stereo quality varies. Some have navigation systems and some are Bluetooth-ready. The question becomes: which equipment am I willing to pay extra for?

After a while, I was tempted to believe that I deserved or needed certain features. What if I get lost? Shouldn't I have a GPS for safety? When I have to leave my car outside overnight, shouldn't I be have an efficient way to heat my posterior? And if fresh air is so good for me, doesn't it make sense to let more of it in through the sun roof? Please. It's not like we get enough sunny days here in the Pacific Northwest to let the sun in anyway.

Word Sparks

Do you know what that attitude is called? It's called entitlement. If you listen to talk radio or have teenagers, you might be familiar with this concept. It's the idea that, by virtue of my very existence, I am entitled to certain rights, possessions, or comfort. We hope our kids grow out of it and it's not a biblical value. But it is in our human, carnal nature to want more. And to think we should get it. And if we're Christians, we sometimes think God owes us.

He doesn't.

Look at this passage from Paul's letter to the Corinthian Christians, as he describes what we've already been given:

"...in him you have been enriched in every way--in all your speaking and in all your knowledge--because our testimony about Christ was confirmed in you. Therefore you do not lack any spiritual gift as you eagerly wait for our Lord Jesus Christ to be revealed. He will keep you strong to the end, so that you will be blameless on the day of our Lord Jesus Christ. God, who has called you into

fellowship with his Son Jesus Christ our Lord, is faithful." (1 Corinthians 1:5-9)

Huh. We have been enriched in every way. We do not lack any spiritual gift. In other words, spiritually speaking, we are fully loaded. *Every* and *any* are pretty absolute words. And, lest we forget, these blessings are brought to you by our Lord and Savior, Jesus Christ. At no cost to us. It cost Him His life.

So what difference does that make in the life of a believer? How does it change our attitudes and behaviors to know that we are fully equipped to live the life He's called us to live?

For one, I think we can walk with a profound sense of freedom and confidence. We are complete. Our security and identity rest in our God, who cannot be shaken and to whom all creation belongs and submits. He will make us and keep us strong. He will empower us to speak words of truth and encouragement.

Secondly, I hope it tweaks our priorities as we remember that we have already been given more than we deserve and our focus should be on pleasing, thanking, and living in wholehearted devotion to the One who gave it to us.

Lastly, we can remember that if we don't have it, we don't need it. God is sovereign and generous in His loving provision.

We can be encouraged by the fact that God has indeed "blessed us in the heavenly realms with every spiritual blessing in Christ". (Ephesians 1:3) We are complete and fully equipped to live for Him. Lord, let it be so. Amen.

Big Leaf, Little Leaf

While out walking one day, enjoying the brisk fall air and clearing my head, I came across numerous leaves that had already made their autumn descent to the pavement. One particularly brilliant Japanese maple caused me to stop. It seemed to be more tenacious than the surrounding trees in the neighborhood in holding on to its foliage. While most of the other trees were almost bare, this stubborn and beautiful display of gold and red was only beginning to let go of last season.

As I looked more closely at the ground, I saw that these delicate leaves were exactly the same shape as the enormous leaves of a large maple I had just passed. A tiny, dainty version of the original.

Just like us.

We are made in God's image. He's the original and we were created to be like Him from the beginning of the creation process.

25 God made the wild animals according to their kinds, the livestock according to their kinds, and all the creatures that move along the ground according to their kinds. And God saw that it was good. ²⁶ Then God said, "Let us make mankind in our image, in our likeness, so that they may rule over the fish in the sea and the birds in the sky, over the livestock and all the wild animals, and over all the creatures that move along the ground."²⁷ So God created mankind in his own image, in the image of God he created them; male and female he created them. (Genesis 1:25-27)

Just like the little maple leaf resembles the big maple leaf, we were knit together in our mother's womb to be a unique and beautiful representation of God's workmanship. (Psalm 139, Ephesians 2:10) We will never be just like God, but there is definitely a family resemblance. As we allow the Holy Spirit to cultivate in us the fruit He wants to grow, people around us will notice the similarities between us and our Father.

We can show love like God. We can be kind. We can sacrifice for others. We can show compassion. So, although, we will never share God's qualities like omniscience or omnipotence, we can look for and emulate those qualities that are within reach and can grow by the power of the Holy Spirit. In so doing, we show the world what God looks like and how He cares for those He created to be in relationship with Him.

Knowing that we are made in God's image also reminds us that when we're unhappy with life's circumstances or relationships in our lives, we are the ones who must adjust to the Maker. God doesn't adjust to us. If He did, He would lose one of His unique characteristics--His immutability - and then He wouldn't be God.

While necessary to the Christian's growth and sanctification process, adjusting to God's perspective isn't easy. But it's crucial to living the abundant life that Jesus promised those who follow Him. When we continually surrender our wills to His and ask Him to examine and transform our hearts, we sense His Presence and we receive strength, wisdom, grace, and mercy to live the life He's called us to live.

He's the big leaf. We're the little leaves.

And when we're connected to our Father, the world will see the resemblance and He can show the world His glory.

Responding to God

When my son was a teenager, I began to discover that the tone and the words he used in responding to me had more to do with his emotions and circumstances than what I had actually said in addressing him. I can't be alone in this epiphany, right? I've heard teenagers can be emotionally capricious.

But it also made me think about my own responses. Both to other people and to God when I'm approached. Why can the same words that brought enlightenment one day bring me to tears another? While it's possible that perimenopausal women can be emotionally capricious, too, I'm thinking it also has something to do with the state of my heart, i.e. whether I'm humbly seeking God and His glory or if I'm wearing myself out with my own agenda.

In reading through the gospel of Luke, I was struck by these very different responses to God's activity in someone's life. Admittedly, I found a little of myself in each of them and I wonder if you might, too.

Word Sparks

[19] But when John rebuked Herod the tetrarch because of his marriage to Herodias, his brother's wife, and all the other evil things he had done, [20] Herod added this to them all: He locked John up in prison. (Luke 3:19-20)

[38] Jesus left the synagogue and went to the home of Simon. Now Simon's mother-in-law was suffering from a high fever, and they asked Jesus to help her. [39] So he bent over her and rebuked the fever, and it left her. She got up at once and began to wait on them. (Luke 4:38-39)

[1] One day as Jesus was standing by the Lake of Gennesaret, the people were crowding around him and listening to the word of God. [2] He saw at the water's edge two boats, left there by the fishermen, who were washing their nets. [3] He got into one of the boats, the one belonging to Simon, and asked him to put out a little from shore. Then he sat down and taught the people from the boat.

[4] When he had finished speaking, he said to Simon, "Put out into deep water, and let down the nets for a catch."

[5] Simon answered, "Master, we've worked hard all

Word Sparks

night and haven't caught anything. But because you say so, I will let down the nets."

6 When they had done so, they caught such a large number of fish that their nets began to break. 7 So they signaled their partners in the other boat to come and help them, and they came and filled both boats so full that they began to sink.

8 When Simon Peter saw this, he fell at Jesus' knees and said, "Go away from me, Lord; I am a sinful man!" 9 For he and all his companions were astonished at the catch of fish they had taken, 10 and so were James and John, the sons of Zebedee, Simon's partners.

Then Jesus said to Simon, "Don't be afraid; from now on you will fish for people." 11 So they pulled their boats up on shore, left everything and followed him. (Luke 5:1-11)

In these passages from the gospel of Luke we see three varying responses to God's activity in someone's life. Herod was rebuked by John concerning his illicit relationship with his brother's wife and he had John put in prison. Later, when he is besotted by this same woman's daughter, he agrees to have John put to death. (Matthew 14:1-12) Herod seems resistant to God's movement in his life, to say the least. It might be more accurate to say that he's immune to it and goes to any length to quiet the voices God sends to bring him to repentance.

Simon's mother was one of many who were physically touched and healed by Jesus when He walked the earth. Her response? She got up at once and began to wait on them. Was this a mere adherence to the accepted customs of the time? Or was it her worshipful response, out of gratitude and understanding, to having God come into her life and relieve her suffering? Was her spontaneous action directly related to her comprehension of the One who had come into her life and responded to her needs?

And what about Simon Peter? This sometimes impetuous, passionate man made his living as a fisherman, going out nightly, looking for a catch to bring in some money. After one of these nights he's approached by Jesus, who tells him to go out into "deep water." Different water than Peter had just been in? Or just to try the same thing again with a new attitude? Peter is dubious but has enough faith to try. What he brings in from his act of faith blows away all his preconceived notions and parameters of Jesus' identity, and it forces Peter to ask for help to carry the abundance Jesus has provided. His response? "Go away from me, Lord; I am a sinful man!" In other words, Peter has not only caught boatloads of fish; he's also caught a glimpse of who Jesus is and who he is in comparison to Him. God's power and holiness have been revealed and so has Peter's sin.

How do I respond to God's movement in my life? When I'm rebuked or when I hear the Holy Spirit whisper words of clear conviction to my heart, do I run or do I embrace the message? When a trusted friend challenges my motivation, do I resist or do I lay it before God and ask Him to reveal the truth so I can be further transformed into His image? Is my consistent response to Jesus' healing Presence in my life to give Him everything in worshipful service? Or do I hold back because I place too high a priority on my comfort and my agenda? Does my understanding of God's holiness cause me to fall on my knees in humility when I realize the depth of my sin? Am I even willing to look at it?

Most of us won't go to Herod's extremes in his desire to cover or justify his sin. But we may go about it in more subtle and socially acceptable ways. Spending less time or sharing less personal information with people who won't let us get away with it is one way. We may also just tweak the story a tad to paint ourselves in more flattering light. Sometimes the temptation is to silence the one trying to point out truth by defending ourselves or accusing, maligning or lashing out at them. Purposeful alienation or misrepresentation stems from the same place Herod's actions did: placing a higher priority on self than on God's truth.

Conversely, what if we took a page from Simon's family book and responded to God's activity in our life--

pleasant or not--by looking at our own sin and humbling ourselves in His Presence, worshipping Him in reverence and awe? The process may be painful as we turn our gaze inward so that we can be freed to respond to God with abandon. But the end result will always be deeper understanding, relationship, and transformation. What wouldn't I do to get to that place?

Word Sparks

Mountaintop Experiences

Have you ever experienced something so profound or so powerful that it changed you, but you were alone so you had to try to articulate that experience to someone else? It can be frustrating or it can help you relive the encounter by telling the story. Often we may find ourselves using phrases like, "I just can't describe to you how beautiful is was!" Even as we're trying to do just that!

Moses and the apostle John lived this scenario and we have it in writing, in the Bible. So, I guess their frustration really proved worth their while since we can know *exactly* what happened, huh?

Still, when we have an encounter with God--a vision, a tender moment, a particular conviction, or insight--it's possible to feel frustration that others have not, or are not currently, experiencing the same things with God. How do we respond to the realization that others are not moving in the direction or at the pace God has us moving?

Here's how it played out for Moses in the desert after

his literal mountaintop experience with God. The story is found in the book of Exodus and the following chapters describe Moses' conversation with God:

Chapter 19 - Moses goes up and down Mount Sinai as an intermediary between the Israelites and God as they promise to consecrate themselves and obey whatever they're told.

Chapter 20 - God speaks loudly, with thunder and lightning, to everyone from Mount Sinai and gives them the Ten Commandments to live by. Then Moses approaches God, who is in a thick darkness.

Chapters 21-23 - God gives Moses further instructions for the social functioning of the Hebrew people.

Chapter 24 - Moses, Joshua and seventy-two elders approach the mountain to worship God. Then Moses and Joshua come a little further. Finally Moses goes alone to the top of the mountain where God is perceived to be "like a consuming fire on the top of the mountain."

Word Sparks

Chapters 25-31 - Moses receives very specific instructions about the materials and construction of the tabernacle, as well as the priests' anointing and wardrobe.

Chapter 32 - Moses descends Mount Sinai, head full of visions and heart full of the experience he's just had with God, when what does he find? His own people dancing around a golden calf they've made because they needed a god and Moses was just taking too long, thank you very much.

When I used to read this story, like so many other accounts in the Bible, I would wonder how the people could be so stupid to miss God when He was right there in their midst. They had been trembling in their sandals a few chapters earlier, promising to follow God and obey His commands, no matter what. No we find them worshipping a golden idol they've specifically been told not to make or worship!

Then I realized that the Israelites hadn't heard or seen anything I'd just read! Moses alone was chosen to receive the Law and communicate it to the Israelites. He had had the sweet communion with God; they hadn't. He'd heard the wonders of the tabernacle and how amazing it was going to be to house His holy Presence; they hadn't.

I don't know about you, but I've been on both sides of this story.

I've been on retreats where I felt the presence of God and heard His voice powerfully. I've walked with God (or He's walked with me) through seasons of intimacy and conviction, where He has transformed me into what I'm becoming. And my frustration at others who aren't experiencing it has been palpable. And that frustration can spill into judgment and anger when others don't want to--or aren't capable of--going where I've been with God. It seems that may have been what happened in Moses in chapter 32. In the end it turns out his anger mirrored God's, but it did cost him another trip up the mountain to replace the stones he broke in his rage.

Other times I get impatient with God and decide for

myself that if He's not going to act in my time frame, I'll just help myself to an idol and move on. And just like Aaron and the others, I find ways to rationalize my behavior and make myself feel better about my disobedience. Aaron told Moses, "You know how prone these people are to evil...they gave me the gold, and I threw it in the fire, and out came this calf!" Right....

The crucial thing to remember is that God is moving each of us along our journey with Him individually and uniquely, even as we function in interdependent community. My faith walk has an effect on others, but it is not the same for everyone. If I'm experiencing a season of conviction and repentance as God reveals Himself to me as holy and mighty, I must fight the urge to respond in contempt to a brother or sister whose heart is full with the joy of blessing and bountiful times. And vice versa.

Our litmus test must always be Scripture and the Holy Spirit's conviction. I can learn from others' seasons and the truth they learn from God, but I don't need to have an identical conviction. I need to depend on God alone for that, and He will take me precisely where I need to go, when I need to go there.

- Take some time this week to read the whole story: Exodus 20-33. What observations or convictions do you have?
- What are you experiencing currently? Hearing from God but frustrated that others don't get it? Or feeling the tug of the Holy Spirit, pushing you toward repentance in an area you're rationalizing?

No Longer a Burden

As I've been engaged in a struggle recently to come to terms with some familiar and hated sin in my life, I was struck by the verse of my favorite hymn. I'd been feeling exhausted from the struggle of continual surrender to the Lord and I cried out to Him to change my heart--one more time. Then these words came to me in the shower:

> *My sin, O the bliss of this glorious thought*
> *My sin, not in part, but the whole*
> *Is nailed to the cross and **I bear it no more***
> *Praise the Lord, Praise the Lord, O My soul!*

It occurred to me that I don't have to bear the constant weight of my sin; that's precisely what Christ died for! He is my Savior, my Healer and my Intercessor. The Holy Spirit will convict me and transform me as I surrender to His convictions and rely on Jesus' sacrifice and the power of the resurrection to change me once again.

I'm not after behavior modification here; I'm after

complete and radical transformation into the image of Christ. I will not brush my sinful responses to life under the proverbial carpet, grieving the Holy Spirit by my refusal to call my sin what it is. I will not grit my teeth and attempt to walk in Pharisaical adherence to regulations and expectations. I will not blame other people or my circumstances for my sinful attitudes.

I will examine my life in the light of the truth--the person of Jesus Christ. I will lay down my pride and admit when I'm wrong. I will fall on my face, at the feet of Jesus, again and again, until He takes me home and I will be like Him.

My sin is nailed to the cross and I bear it no more! Praise the Lord, praise the Lord, O my soul!

Setting The Pace

When my son was 14, he ran in his first 5K race. He placed 67th out of 966 runners. As pleased as he was with his finish, he was a little disappointed in his time. He was hoping to shave a bit off his last time, but he ended up actually adding some time. Instead of the wooded trails where his high school cross country practiced and meets were, this was a 5K along the streets of town, along the same trail as the 10K run, which had started earlier, and adjacent to the miniature loop of the kids' 1K dash. It was more like a festival atmosphere than a pure athletic event.

In the car after the race he talked about the reasons for his slower time. He seemed to think it had a lot to do with the wide variety of people running and the lack of someone he could use as a pacesetter for himself. Like my friend when she drives, Charlie likes to pick out a fast runner ahead of him and make it his goal to pass him. The challenge forces him to push himself to run faster. And today he couldn't find his guy.

Word Sparks

So, what do exceptional runners do? The ones who actually *win* races like this one? Charlie says they pace themselves. Now, that's a good idea! Then it doesn't matter who runs with you, where you run, or how many people there are.

Wait, is there a spiritual application here? I think so.

There are lots of decisions we have to make every day about how to live out our faith. Many of these decisions can be made almost intuitively if we know Scripture and are actively pursuing our relationship with God by listening to the Holy Spirit's promptings. Sometimes, however, we hit a wall. A relationship unravels. Plans don't come to fruition. We lose our way. Our friends and leaders are giving mixed advice and viewpoints.

Who, then, becomes our pacesetter for living out our Christian faith uniquely as God created each of us to do?

When we go through life on spiritual autopilot or depending on others for wisdom without going to the Source of wisdom and guidance, we run the risk of

Word Sparks

running the race without a pace set for us. Then it's too easy to fall behind and forget the reason we're running.

Instead, we would do well to follow the suggestion of the writer of Hebrews, who wrote, *"...let us run with perseverance the race marked out for us."* (Hebrews 12:1) Let's follow Jesus, keeping pace with Him and listening to His voice as we run our race. Then, when friends disagree or we find ourselves in a situation where the answer or the comfort we seek isn't quick in coming, we know who to follow.

The Holy Spirit's job description includes being a Counselor to convict of guilt and sin and righteousness, and to remind us of everything that Jesus taught. (John 16) When we listen to that voice, running to God to find grace and mercy in our time of need, we can find Him, Who is our Way. Then, regardless of the outcome of our situation, when we find God, we win.

Word Sparks

City Moses and Desert Moses

Does writing about a proverbial desert experience seem trite? What if it's only coincidental that one of the locations in the story happens to be a desert?

Not long ago, I was struck by so many life lesson scenarios in the life of Moses as I read the familiar story that I had to pause and dig into at least one. There may be more, I should warn you.

As you may recall from the book of Exodus, Moses had a life split into three parts, each part lasting approximately forty years. The first forty were as a Prince of Egypt (we've all seen the movie), the second forty were as a shepherd for his father-in-law in the Midian desert, and the last forty years he spent leading a million or so cranky Hebrews out of Egypt and into the land God had promised. There you go. Exodus in a nutshell.

What's interesting is that the first forty years of Moses' life are covered in Chapters 1 and 2, the next forty in chapters 2-4, and the last forty years are stretched out between the last 36 chapters of Exodus, plus the entire books of Leviticus, Numbers, and Deuteronomy. I guess those are the ones we're meant to pay close attention to.

But there is something significant in the experiences that get merely a brief summary in the beginning of "the real story." Where Moses came from. His first eighty years of life were a very long preparation period for the history-altering later years in that God used his experiences as a royal prince in a fertile land and as a family desert shepherd to launch him into those final challenging years as the leader of God's chosen people.

After a dramatic discovery as a baby in a basket by Pharaoh's daughter, Moses was raised as a rich and privileged prince in an area of Egypt that was green and lush and filled with all the trappings of a powerful kingdom. According to ancient Egyptian religious beliefs, Moses' adoptive grandfather, the Pharaoh, would have been considered to hold absolute power over a vast empire, but he would have also shared deity with a host of Egyptian gods and goddesses, thereby serving as a sort of liaison between the human and divine worlds.

After murdering an Egyptian in a fit of righteous anger, Moses flees this life of luxury and finds a safe haven with people in the desert of Midian, just south of the land that the Israelites eventually settled under the leadership of Joshua. But that's for another day.

In the desert of Midian, Moses spent a few decades with his father-in-law's sheep, in the desert, learning how to work for himself, learning about nature, spending some quality time in solitude. He may have thought about his previous life in Egypt, when he was surrounded by temples and verdant landscapes by the Nile. He was assimilating and going through a radical re-identification process. From clean-shaven prince to hirsute shepherd. From a life of leisure to a daily search for water and concern for safety.

Meanwhile, back in Egypt...

Exodus 2:23-25 tells us what was happening while Moses was adjusting to his new identity:

23 During that long period, the king of Egypt died. The

Israelites groaned in their slavery and cried out, and their cry for help because of their slavery went up to God. 24 God heard their groaning and he remembered his covenant with Abraham, with Isaac and with Jacob. 25 So God looked on the Israelites and was concerned about them.

The Israelites groaned and cried out. God heard them and was concerned about them.

While Moses was in the desert learning to be a new person, his people were straining under the weight of their servitude, and God was about to do something on a miraculous scale for their deliverance and His ultimate glory.

Now comes the part we can all relate to.

It's a little thing I like to call perspective.

There was no way for Moses or the Israelites in Egypt to know the exact timing that God was going to put His plan in motion. But God did. There is no way for us to know when our present circumstances will change and God will spring into action in a totally unexpected--or perhaps long-awaited fashion. But He does.

That's what sovereign means. God is always aware of and in control of plans and purposes for His people.

Life not moving toward your dreams as fast as you'd like? Are you suffering under unbearable circumstances? God knows and He is working out His plan exactly as He designed it, whether we're aware of the moving parts or not.

Tragic phone call? Bad news from the doctor? Unexpected turn of events that has your head spinning? Just like God looked at the Israelites and was concerned, He knows your situation and He is concerned for you.

For all we know, we are sitting right where Moses and the Israelites were: separated from our ultimate destiny, but on the brink of participating in God's glorious plans. And the best thing we can do, over and over again, is cry out to Him and press into Him. Because when we get more of God, then the waiting is bearable. The suffering is tolerable. We can breathe through the tragic and be grounded amid the crashing waves. And what He's about to do is nothing short of amazing.

Word Sparks

- Read Exodus 1-2. Which scenes or characters do you relate to? How can you move closer to God in your situation?
- Read Psalm 18:1-6. Have you experienced what the psalmist has written about? Can you declare with assurance that the LORD is your rock, your fortress, and your deliverer? Verses 1-3 might be good ones to memorize.
- Read Romans 8:18-39. What comfort do you receive from these verses if you belong to Christ? How does it give you perspective in your current situation?

Connect with Jenni

Jenni's latest blogs and speaking engagements can be found at TheWordSpark.com. Follow her on Twitter at @JWordspark, or email her at jenni@thewordspark.com for information on speaking at one of your upcoming events.

Made in the USA
Middletown, DE
30 June 2015